Instant Edmodo How-to

Implement a learning management system in your classroom environment seamlessly and engage students in their own learning with Edmodo

Dayna Laur

PUBLISHING

BIRMINGHAM - MUMBAI

Instant Edmodo How-to

First published: June 2013

Production Reference: 1170613

Published by Packt Publishing Ltd.
Livery Place
35 Livery Street
Birmingham B3 2PB, UK.

ISBN 978-1-84969-730-9

www.packtpub.com

Credits

Author
Dayna Laur

Reviewer
Kristyn A. Kamps

Acquisition Editor
Joanne Fitzpatrick

Commissioning Editor
Yogesh Dalvi

Technical Editor
Amit Ramadas

Project Coordinator
Akash Poojary

Proofreader
Mario Cecere

Production Coordinator
Conidon Miranda

Cover Work
Conidon Miranda

About the Author

Dayna Laur is a veteran high school social studies teacher of 14 years where she has implemented numerous authentic learning experiences in her co-taught special education classes, advanced placement courses, and mainstream social studies classes. During her teaching tenure she has been featured in Edutopia's Schools That Work series and as a model teacher for authentic learning as produced by the National Institute for Professional Practice.

She currently serves as a Senior National Faculty member for the Buck Institute for Education and travels nationally to train teachers on effective implementation of project-based learning.

She has a BA in History from VA Tech, a MEd in Curriculum and Instruction from the University of Pittsburgh, and a MSEd in 21st Century Teaching and Learning from Wilkes University. She is also a two-time National Board Certified teacher. She has written articles that have appeared in Tech-Edge and EARCOS Journal. She has a full-length publication entitled *Authentic Learning Experiences: A Real-World Approach to Project Based Learning*. In addition to authentic learning experiences, Dayna's educational interests include the implementation of the Common Core Standards and technology integration. You can follow her on Twitter @daylynn. This is her first book with Packt Publishing.

About the Reviewer

Kristyn A. Kamps currently teaches 7th and 8th grade science in Holland, Michigan. Six years ago, when her district implemented a one-to-one laptop program, Kristyn helped pioneer strategies for deepening student understanding in a one-to-one learning environment using project-based learning as the structural framework.

Through her commitment to teacher excellence, Kristyn facilitated K-8 restructuring of science curriculum to align with state and national standards. In addition, she has helped develop curriculum for science, English, literature, technology and culture courses that incorporate universal design for learning components and 21st century skills through the use of technological applications, such as Edmodo. As a National Faculty member of the Buck Institute for Education, Kristyn has also led professional development workshops on one-to-one laptop implementation and project-based learning at district and state education conferences.

She received her B.A. in elementary education from Calvin College in Grand Rapids, MI, with a social studies composite concentration and an emphasis on psychology and history. English was her subject minor. Her degree has given her experience teaching 2nd, 3rd, 6th, 7th, and 8th grades over the past 26 years. During her graduate studies, she focused on gifted and talented education, educational technology and science, math, and technology education.

> I would like to thank my dear friend and colleague, Dayna Laur, for involving me in this project. As always, it has been a pleasure to work together!

www.PacktPub.com

Support files, eBooks, discount offers and more

You might want to visit www.PacktPub.com for support files and downloads related to your book.

Did you know that Packt offers eBook versions of every book published, with PDF and ePub files available? You can upgrade to the eBook version at www.PacktPub.com and as a print book customer, you are entitled to a discount on the eBook copy. Get in touch with us at service@packtpub.com for more details.

At www.PacktPub.com, you can also read a collection of free technical articles, sign up for a range of free newsletters and receive exclusive discounts and offers on Packt books and eBooks.

http://PacktLib.PacktPub.com

Do you need instant solutions to your IT questions? PacktLib is Packt's online digital book library. Here, you can access, read and search across Packt's entire library of books.

Why Subscribe?

- ▶ Fully searchable across every book published by Packt
- ▶ Copy and paste, print and bookmark content
- ▶ On demand and accessible via web browser

Free Access for Packt account holders

If you have an account with Packt at www.PacktPub.com, you can use this to access PacktLib today and view nine entirely free books. Simply use your login credentials for immediate access.

Table of Contents

Preface

Welcome to *Instant Edmodo How-to*. In this book, we will navigate the steps needed to seamlessly implement this learning management system in your classroom environment. Whether you are a novice or have dabbled with Edmodo, this book will teach you the tips and tricks to successfully use all the features of the system. You will walk away with the tools necessary to better engage your students in their own learning.

What this book covers

Setting up your profile (Simple) explains why setting up your profile is one of the most important steps in starting your Edmodo experience. This recipe also covers how your profile gives others insight into the professional you, as you will want to provide a snapshot of your educational expertise.

Creating Edmodo groups (Simple) covers the process to create groups in Edmodo. This recipe also talks about organizing your students into manageable groups, which can be maintained, archived, or deleted in future school years.

Creating student accounts (Simple) explains the process to create student accounts once the groups have been created.

Maintaining Edmodo online safety (Simple) explains the importance of maintaining online safety of students, although online classroom environments are perfect for teaching digital safety. This recipe also discusses a few tips to ensure students' Edmodo experience is a safe one.

Creating small groups (Intermediate) explains the necessity to break a full class into smaller sections for a variety of tasks, which will allow you to quickly and easily maneuver students into an array of smaller groups.

Posting on the Edmodo wall (Simple) explains the importance of wall feeds. The feed on Edmodo is similar to that of Facebook. If you are a Facebook user, you will find Edmodo to be an easy transition.

Creating and editing assignments (Intermediate) covers the importance of paperless assignments. You can upload documents, link videos, and assign due dates to help keep your students on track.

Creating quizzes (Intermediate) explains how to create a multiple choice, short answer, true or false, fill in the blank, or matching quiz that can be shared to multiple classes and scored by Edmodo. The results will be displayed as a graph to help you determine any deficient areas of learning.

Using the Edmodo gradebook (Intermediate) explains Edmodo gradebook, which is a scoring method in Edmodo. The use of the Edmodo gradebook will give parents and students immediate online access to their class standings and progress.

Managing your Edmodo planner (Simple) talks about Edmodo's easy-to-reference calendar for teachers, student, and parents. You don't have to worry about students forgetting to write assignment due dates in their planner anymore.

Managing your Edmodo Library (Intermediate) talks about the Edmodo Library that maintains a virtual record of all of your documents, links, and videos. This recipe also explains how to organize your content and share it with others.

Creating parent accounts in Edmodo (Intermediate) talks about giving parents access to your classroom group, which creates a connected experience for them. Parent accounts are automatically linked to the appropriate students by Edmodo, so take advantage of this feature.

Participating in Edmodo communities (Intermediate) talks about using Edmodo to help you grow your personal learning network. Connect with your subject area and then find additional communities of interest with which you can engage to find resources, share ideas, and receive feedback on your work.

Using Edmodo apps (Advanced) discusses the apps available on the Edmodo app store. The basic functions of Edmodo are free. Once you've mastered the ins and outs of the tools, you may be ready for the more advanced, paid offerings that can be downloaded from the Edmodo app store.

What you need for this book

To use Edmodo, you simply need an Internet connection. Edmodo is a Web 2.0 tool designed for educators, so you also need to have an affiliation with an educational organization in order to create a valid Edmodo account.

Who this book is for

This book is for educators who intend to use Edmodo for instructional support in classrooms or in professional development sessions.

Conventions

In this book, you will find a number of styles of text that distinguish between different kinds of information. Here are some examples of these styles, and an explanation of their meaning.

Code words in text are shown as follows: "If you are going to leave the newly restored group open for any length of time, you may wish to change the group name by simply adding the word `Closed`."

New terms and **important words** are shown in bold. Words that you see on the screen, in menus or dialog boxes for example, appear in the text like this: "Click on **I'm a Teacher**."

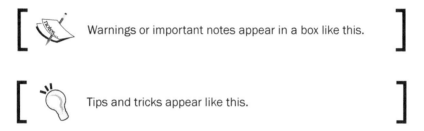

Warnings or important notes appear in a box like this.

Tips and tricks appear like this.

Reader feedback

Feedback from our readers is always welcome. Let us know what you think about this book—what you liked or may have disliked. Reader feedback is important for us to develop titles that you really get the most out of.

To send us general feedback, simply send an e-mail to feedback@packtpub.com, and mention the book title via the subject of your message.

If there is a topic that you have expertise in and you are interested in either writing or contributing to a book, see our author guide on www.packtpub.com/authors.

Customer support

Now that you are the proud owner of a Packt book, we have a number of things to help you to get the most from your purchase.

Errata

Although we have taken every care to ensure the accuracy of our content, mistakes do happen. If you find a mistake in one of our books—maybe a mistake in the text or the code—we would be grateful if you would report this to us. By doing so, you can save other readers from frustration and help us improve subsequent versions of this book. If you find any errata, please report them by visiting http://www.packtpub.com/submit-errata, selecting your book, clicking on the **errata submission form** link, and entering the details of your errata. Once your errata are verified, your submission will be accepted and the errata will be uploaded on our website, or added to any list of existing errata, under the Errata section of that title. Any existing errata can be viewed by selecting your title from http://www.packtpub.com/support.

Piracy

Piracy of copyright material on the Internet is an ongoing problem across all media. At Packt, we take the protection of our copyright and licenses very seriously. If you come across any illegal copies of our works, in any form, on the Internet, please provide us with the location address or website name immediately so that we can pursue a remedy.

Please contact us at copyright@packtpub.com with a link to the suspected pirated material.

We appreciate your help in protecting our authors, and our ability to bring you valuable content.

Questions

You can contact us at questions@packtpub.com if you are having a problem with any aspect of the book, and we will do our best to address it.

Instant Edmodo How-to

Welcome to *Instant Edmodo How-to*. In this book, you will navigate the steps needed to seamlessly implement this learning management system in your classroom environment. Whether you are a novice or have dabbled with Edmodo, this book will teach you the tips and tricks to successfully use all of the features of the system. You will walk away with the tools necessary to better engage your students in their own learning.

Setting up your profile (Simple)

While it may seem trivial, setting up your profile is one of the most important steps in starting your Edmodo experience. Your profile gives others insight into the professional you! Remember that the users on Edmodo are fellow teachers, and the ability to connect with these educators around the world is an opportunity that should not be overlooked. Thus, it is important to take care to provide a snapshot of your educational expertise.

Getting ready

Create your teacher account at `http://www.edmodo.com`.

How to do it...

Creating an Edmodo account only takes minutes, but is the most important step as you begin your Edmodo journey.

1. Click on **I'm a Teacher**.
2. Choose a username and password.
3. Connect to your educational institution to verify your teacher account.
4. Upload a photo of yourself.
5. Join online Edmodo communities (available now, but advisable to skip at this juncture).
6. Find teacher connections.
7. Fill in your **About Me** section.

How it works...

The Edmodo website looks like the following:

On the Edmodo home page, `http://edmodo.com`, click on **I'm a Teacher** to begin your Edmodo journey. Set up your teacher account by using a unique username and a password that you can remember. If your first choice of username is not available, please choose another until you are notified of a successful selection. The e-mail address that you attach to your Edmodo account should be your school e-mail. You will also need to choose your school affiliation at this time. If your school is not listed as a choice on Edmodo, you may do a manual search for your school. Selecting your school will ensure that fellow teachers within your district can easily connect with you. This also provides Edmodo with the background to be able to make suggestions on other educators with whom you may want to connect. Additionally, once you become active in the Edmodo community, your school selection will provide better insight into your teaching background, and will provide a greater context for other teachers to potentially partner with you in collaborative endeavors.

Once you have created your account, you will be prompted to upload a photo of yourself. This is advisable in order to make you easier to distinguish when you interact in the professional communities, and it literally puts a face to your name. Certainly you have the option of using one of Edmodo's generic pictures. However, you will inevitably be sharing this generic picture with thousands of other users. You will be prompted to create a unique URL. This will provide additional ease to search for you when making professional connections. Your username is probably the easiest option for this.

Next, you have the option of joining an array of online professional communities. We will come back to this step later in the section on Edmodo Communities. However, you will notice that Edmodo has automatically enrolled you in their **Help** community. This community is designated with the question mark symbol and once you have been redirected to your home page, you will notice it located in the left section of your screen, directly below your established **Groups**.

From your profile page, you can find teacher connections. You can choose from the teacher suggestions made by Edmodo. Edmodo makes these connection suggestions based on your school district selection. These suggestions are located on the left-hand side of the profile screen. Simply click on a teacher with whom you would like to make a connection. If you would like to connect to other teachers who are not on Edmodo, you may send them an invitation from your profile page. Simply hover over the link **How to improve my profile?** that is located on the right-hand side of the screen. From here, enter the e-mail addresses of those educators you would like to join Edmodo.

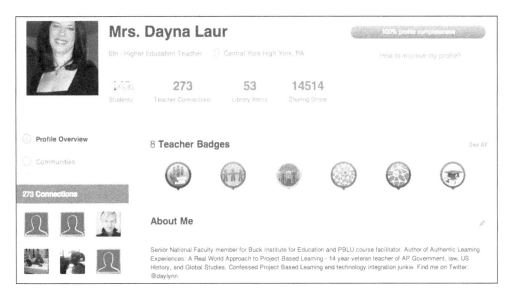

Your profile page also provides you with the ability to write an **About Me** description. In this portion, include the courses you teach and any educational interests you might have that could potentially pique the interest of your fellow educators. Note my personal Edmodo **About Me** description as seen in the preceding screenshot.

There's more...

You have created the basics of your profile. However, in order to gain clout in the Edmodo online community, you may want to begin earning badges. Your first chance to do so is in your profile setting.

Earning teacher badges

You will notice on your Edmodo profile page that you have the opportunity to earn teacher badges. Simply having your teacher account verified as being one that belongs to an educator will earn you the **Verified Teacher** badge. However, you can collect many others. Joining one of the subject area communities will net you a **Community Member** badge and following a publisher community will score you the **Publisher Collaborator** badge. Connect to at least 10 other educators on Edmodo and you will find yourself awarded with the **Connected** badge. The more educators with whom you connect, the more ways you can earn differentiated levels of this badge. The other badge you may want to covet earning is your **Librarian** badge. This is possible when you begin sharing resources on Edmodo that other educators find to be useful. (See **Sharing Resources** for additional information on how to do so.)

Creating Edmodo groups (Simple)

You are ready to begin using Edmodo with your students. You may create as many groups as needed to match the number of classes you teach. These groups may be maintained, archived, or deleted in future school years.

Getting ready

Determine the number of classes that you would like to establish on Edmodo.

How to do it...

Creating groups is a simple process.

1. Click on **Create**.
2. Name your group.
3. Select a **Grade** level or **Range**.
4. Select a **Subject Area**.
5. Click on **Create**.

How it works...

After completing your profile, you can navigate to your home page by clicking on the house icon on the top-left section of your screen. Look to the left of your screen. You will see the **Join** and **Create** options underneath the **Groups** designation. Click on **Create**.

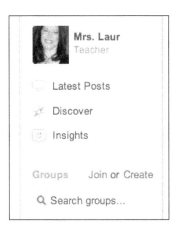

It is now time to designate a group name for your class. You may simply want to call your class by the grade level or course name and specify the school year or semester. For example, `Third Grade 2014` or `Algebra I Spring Semester 2013` would be an appropriate name. If you have multiple courses with the same name, you can further designate the name by using the period in which you teach the class. For example, if you have two Algebra I classes, you may name one group `Algebra I Period 1 2013` and another group might be designated as `Algebra I Period 4 2013`. If needed, these names can be changed in the future by going into your **Group Settings**, which is located on the right-hand side of your home page.

Once you have named your group, you may select a **Grade** level or **Range**. The grade level is more appropriate for elementary and middle school teachers, while the grade range is appropriate for high school teachers who may have more than one grade level represented in a class. Similarly, you will also need to choose a subject area that represents your group. The **Grade** level or **Range** designation, as well as the **Subject Area** designation, is simply a data collection tool for Edmodo at this time. This information can be changed at any time by clicking on **Group Settings** located on the right-hand side of your Edmodo home page.

Now that you have created your group, an automatically generated six-digit group code will be provided. This is located on the right-hand side of you Edmodo home screen. This group code is unique to each group and can be changed or locked as needed. This is the code that will be shared with students so that they may join and begin interacting in your Edmodo group. You will want to lock this group code once all students have joined. Edmodo will automatically lock a code 14 days after a group has been created or the code has been reset.

Please note that Edmodo does not place a limit on the number of groups that you may create. Therefore, there is no need to delete a group after you have finished with the course. It is, however, advisable that you archive your group. This is discussed in the *Archiving your groups* section. Additionally, with the potential to have multiple groups, it is advisable to color code each group. To do this, simply click on the colored square next to the group name on the left-hand side of your Edmodo home page screen. Choose the desired color to be associated with your group.

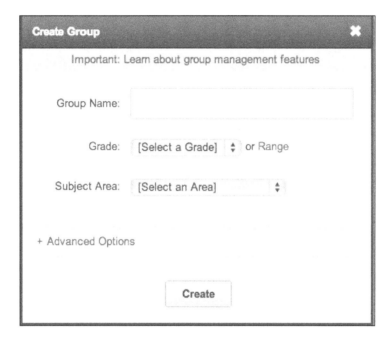

If you are part of a professional development session that is using Edmodo, you may want to join an already established group. This is also true if you are working with another teacher and need to join their already-established class. If this is the case, you will be provided with a group code in order to enter that group. Click on **Join** that is located in the same group area beside the section where you created your groups. Enter the provided code, click on **Join**, and you will automatically be directed to that previously-established group.

There's more...

You may want to customize your group settings in order to better manage and facilitate your newly created groups.

Advanced options

When creating your groups, you will see an **Advanced Options** section under the **Subject Area:** field. Click on **Advanced Options**. You will have the option to choose your settings for student interaction. Click on **Default all new members to read-only** if you would like to have your group participants only consume information that you provide and do not want your participants to be able to post any information in your group. Click on **Moderate all posts and replies** if you want to control what information your group participants post. If you choose this option, no information will be posted to your group without your approval.

In the **Advanced Options** section, you are also able to write a description of your group. You are, however, limited to 260 characters for your description.

Archiving your groups

Once your group is no longer needed, you may delete or archive your group. Simply click on **Group Settings** and click on **Archive Group**. Archiving your group will allow you to maintain the information complied within the group, but will take it away from your list of groups on the left-hand side of your Edmodo home screen. This helps to keep the numbers of groups you maintain manageable. It also will take away the ability of any group members to access the group information. At any time, however, you may restore your group. To do this, simply click on the folder icon at the bottom of your listed groups on the left-hand side of your Edmodo home screen. Your list of archived groups will appear and you may choose any of them to view or to restore. To view, simply click on the group name. To restore, click on the green, curved arrow to the right of the designated group. In order to see the grades of an archived group, you will need to restore the group. If you are going to leave the newly restored group open for any length of time, you may wish to change the group name by simply adding the word `Closed`. This will signal to any group members that the group is no longer active even though the group has been restored.

Adding a co-teacher to the group

Once you have created your group, you are the owner and sole controller of the group. If you would like to add a co-teacher to the group with most of the same privileges as you have, you only need to follow a few simple steps. Provide the co-teacher with the group code. Once the co-teacher has joined the group, click on **Members** located at the top center of your Edmodo home page. Select your co-teacher. The selected member of the group will now appear in a new window on the right-hand side of your screen. Click on **Access** and change the access level to **Co-Teacher**.

Creating student accounts (Simple)

Now that you have created your groups, you need your students to join them. Remember that Edmodo is a secure environment for your students, but you need to take care to follow the steps to ensure the integrity of the groups is maintained.

Getting ready

If you have younger students, or a large class, you may want to enlist the help of an aide to get your student accounts started. Students create individual accounts at `http://www.edmodo.com`.

How to do it...

Have students take these steps to create an Edmodo account.

1. Students should select **I'm a Student**.
2. Type in the teacher-provided group code.
3. Create a username.
4. Create a password.
5. Enter e-mail, if school provides.
6. Enter first and last names.
7. Click on **You and your parent agree to our TOS and our Privacy Policy**.
8. Click on **Sign up**.

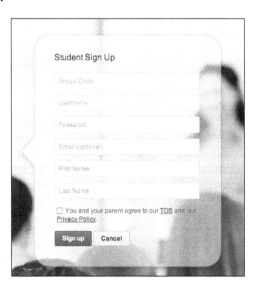

How it works...

Students cannot create an Edmodo account without a teacher-provided group code as created through the steps in the previous section. This is to ensure an added level of safety when students are participating in online activities through Edmodo. This also means that no student can join your group without the group code. It is suggested that once all students join the group, you, the teacher, should lock the group code. To lock the group code, simply click on the black Lock icon located next to the blue box with the white group code. If you unlock the group code, a new code is automatically generated.

It is suggested that students use a school-provided username and password, if one exists. If not, for younger students, it will be helpful for you, the teacher, to create a username and password for each student. Please remember that it is possible that a username will already be taken. If this is the case, simply use a variation of the username until one is accepted.

The **Terms of Service** (**TOS**) and **Privacy Policy** from Edmodo must be agreed to in order to establish an account. It is certainly advisable for you to read these, as there is nothing out of the ordinary from any other online Web 2.0 provider. For your students, as minors, however, it must be noted that parents need to agree to these terms as well. You can create a letter to send home to parents explaining the use of Edmodo in the classroom and request their signature as the acceptance of these terms. Edmodo also has a sample parent letter that can be downloaded from their site in the **Teacher Rollout Resources** section of the **Help Center** section. If your district has a blanket policy that parents sign in at the beginning of the year, this will suffice as well.

If a student already has an Edmodo account from participation in another class, they do not need to set up a new Edmodo account. Have these students log into Edmodo and join your group. Students will need to click on **Join** in the section under **Groups** on the left-hand side of the Edmodo home page. Students will be prompted to enter the unique group code for your class. Once this code has been entered, membership to the group is granted.

There's more...

You may find that you need to remove a student from a group or limit the interaction they may have with other students.

Managing group members

Students can be removed from a group or set to a read-only status at any time. To do this, simply click on **Members** located in the top-center of your Edmodo home screen. Select the student in question. A new window will appear on the right-hand side of your screen. From here, you may choose to remove the selected student or set the student to a read-only status. Setting a student to a read-only status will still allow the student to access content uploaded and posted on Edmodo. That student, however, will not be able to post on Edmodo and thus, the student's interaction on the platform will cease.

Joining the group by URL

If you have locked your group code or do not want to distribute the code to a student who already has an Edmodo account, you can share a link for joining your group. This link is located on the right-hand side of your Edmodo group home page. It is designated in the box under **Join Group URL**. Once a student clicks on the provided link, they will be taken to a screen that asks them to **Send Join Request**. Once the student clicks on this link, the request will be sent to you, the owner of the group. You must approve the request. The **Join Request** option can be found under **Notifications** on the right-hand side of your Edmodo home page in the yellow box. Click on the **Join Request** option and click on **Accept** to have the student formally join your group.

Maintaining Edmodo online safety (Simple)

Online classroom environments are perfect for teaching digital safety. Follow these few tips to ensure that your students' Edmodo experience is a safe one.

Getting ready

Familiarize yourself with the already built-in features that Edmodo has to offer for online safety.

How to do it...

In order to maintain online safety while using Edmodo, follow these simple steps:

1. Lock your group code.
2. Monitor students.
3. Set up a district subdomain.

How it works...

Edmodo is an educational tool and thus, the creators of Edmodo have designed the system with the best interest of your students in mind. However, there are several quick and easy steps to take to ensure that your students' safety is not compromised.

First and foremost, you should never share your group code publically. Do not post the code on your class website. Do not allow your students to share the group code. In fact, as soon as you have your students join the group, lock your code. You can do this by clicking on the padlock symbol on the left-hand side of your main group page. Once you click on this, you will see the words **LOCKED** in the blue shaded area that previously contained your unique group code. If at any time you need to unlock the code, simply click on the drop-down arrow next to the **LOCKED** designation. You may reset your code at that time to allow additional group members to join the group. However, you will need to remember to lock the code again.

Any good teacher knows that even the best students can occasionally be off-task, which might lead to the potential for inappropriate postings. The best way to combat this is to monitor the posts made by students. Each new post or response to a post from the teacher will be highlighted in yellow. A quick glance at these posts will determine if anything inappropriate is listed. As the owner of the group, you will have the ability to delete any post or response to a post that is inappropriate.

Claiming a district subdomain in Edmodo provides an additional layer of online security for your students. To claim your subdomain, have someone from the administration of your district follow the steps at `http://www.edmodo.com/institutions/claims-stage2`. The use of a subdomain ensures that the district administrator verifies a teacher status. Therefore, a student cannot create a teacher profile via a subdomain. The subdomain also allows teachers within the district to easily share resources and the administrator to post notes to the teachers within the school or to the public school page for parents and community members.

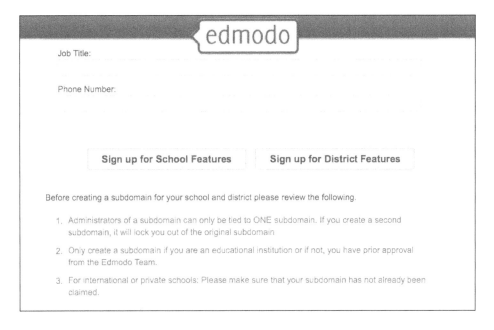

There's more...

If an inappropriate activity is posted on the group's wall, you can limit or remove a member of your group.

Removing group members

To remove a member of your group, click on **Members** at the top of your main group page. Click on the chosen group member's name and click on **Remove from Group** on the right-hand side of the screen. If you do not want to formally remove a member from the group, but want to ensure they cannot post in the group, follow the same procedure as removing a student. However, you will need to click on **Read-Only**.

Creating small groups (Intermediate)

Sometimes is it necessary to break your full class into smaller sections for a variety of tasks. This management feature will allow you to quickly and easily maneuver students into an array of smaller groups.

Getting ready

Determine the number of students per small group and the purpose for creating the small groups.

How to do it...

Create your small groups to manage with these simple steps.

1. Click on **Small Groups**.
2. Click on **New Small Group**.
3. Name your small group.
4. Click on the small group name.
5. Drag the selected group members.

How it works...

Sometimes it is necessary to split students into smaller groups for an assignment, peer reviews, or for additional instructions for those that need review or enrichment. The **Small Group** feature allows you to post, assign, and facilitate these smaller cohorts of students easily. Just click on the **Small Group** tab that is located at the top-center of your Edmodo home group page. Click on **New Small Group** and name it. Choose the specific students from the master list of the group members. These student names will automatically show up on the right-hand side of your screen. You merely need to drag the names of the selected students. If you need to remove a student, click red "X" next to the appropriate name.

The small group will now show up under the main group name on the left-hand side of your Edmodo home page. The small group colors can be changed the same way in which the main group colors are changed. Color coding will help you visually with managing multiple small groups.

Once small groups are created, you will be able to post notes, create assignments, and send quizzes to the appropriately identified small groups. This process mirrors the process described in the upcoming sections.

There's more...

You may only need a small group for a short segment of your class.

Archiving or deleting small groups

Small groups can be deleted or archived just like the main groups. Click on Small Groups at the top-center of the main Edmodo group page. Click on the wheel icon to the far right of the named small group page. Select the appropriate action to archive. To delete the small group, click on red "X" to the right of the wheel. Deleting the small group will lose all of the information associated with it. Archiving the small group will allow you to access the information at a later time.

Posting on the Edmodo wall (Simple)

The feed on Edmodo is similar to that of Facebook. If you are a Facebook user, you will find Edmodo to be an easy transition.

Getting ready

Determine the message you need to post on your wall and to which groups you will need to send the message.

How to do it...

Get ready to post your first message by following these steps:

1. Click on the appropriate type of posting (**Note**, **Alert**, or **Poll**).
2. Type your message.
3. Attach a file, link, or resource from your library.
4. Schedule to post (if needed).
5. Type in the recipients or group to whom you intend to send the post.

How it works...

You can easily send a message to a group, multiple groups, or individual members of a group. Simply click on **Note** and type the message you want to send to your group members. There is no character limit when typing a note. If you need to send something more urgent, you can click on **Alert**. The **Alert** option gives a limit of 140 characters. However, the **Alert** option will signify to your group members a more urgent message. Choose the group or groups that you want to send the note or alert to. The ability to send a note or an alert to multiple groups at once can save you time. Type the message once and distribute it to as many groups as you need.

The **Note** feature permits the creator to upload a file or include a link with the note. A file may be added from your Edmodo Library or directly from your computer. The link is a simple copied and pasted URL with a description of the link. A video link will play directly in Edmodo. All other URLs will link out to the website from Edmodo. The **Alert** feature does not have this capability.

Please keep in mind that sending a note to more than one group could potentially cause a few irritations. Remember that recipients of the note have the ability to respond to the note by using the **Reply** feature once the note (or poll) has been posted. Thus, if you are running several large groups at a time, you will probably want to send a note to each group. This will prevent the replies from getting lost in the shuffle, as it is much easier to manage replies from 30 members in one group than replies from 150 members in multiple groups. It will also help to ensure that your group members are reading the replies posted by their classmates. Students are more likely to read through 30 replies than they are to read through 150 replies.

You may want to create a post in advance without sending it. To do this, click on **Schedule** on the lower-right side under the note. In this screen, you can select the day and time you want to send the post. This is a great feature when you would like to create posts in advance, but do not want the group members to see the posts. You also need to remember that the posts will show up in the feed on the main page of the group in the order in which you post them. That means the first note you create and post will be at the bottom of the news feed order.

If your note or alert contains a mistake that you notice after the post has been made, you still have time to edit the contents of the message. Hover over the post with your cursor and you will notice a small upside down arrow appearing to the top-right of the post. Click on the arrow to reveal a menu of options. These options include the ability to edit or delete a post.

It is also possible to edit a post before it is sent. Go to the yellow-highlighted **Notifications** section on the top right-hand corner of your home screen. Find the desired post by clicking on the **Scheduled Posts** list. All scheduled posts will then be revealed on the main portion of your screen. Find the post and hover over it to reveal the drop-down arrow on the right-hand side of the post. You may choose to **Delete Post**, **Edit Post**, or **Reschedule Post**. Make the appropriate changes and return to your home screen by clicking on the Home icon on the top left-hand side of your screen.

There's more...

You may wish to receive feedback from your group members that can be visually recorded via a poll.

Creating a poll

Click on **Poll** on the main page of your group. Type the question you desire students to answer. Type in the appropriate choices in the areas designated as **answer #_**. Two sections are automatically provided, but you may click on **Add Answer** to increase the number of possible choices for student selection in the poll response. You may immediately post the poll or schedule the post in the same manner as the notes and alerts. Choose the appropriate group from whom you want to elicit responses. Sending the poll to more than one group will increase the number of responses. Once group members begin to respond to the poll, your main group page will update the bar graph of responses by clicking on **Refresh**.

Organizing your posts

Sort your posts by creating a set of tags to track your notes. Once a post has been created, click on the **Tag** icon below the post. Click on **New Tag** and assign a name to the tag. Once tag names have been created, these too will show up in the drop-down **Tag** menu located under each post. To filter your tags, choose the Tag icon at the top of your Edmodo home page. Click on the icon and choose **My Tags**. These tags can be shared with other group members. To share a tag, click on **Shared** from the same tag icon. Click on **Manage Tags**. Highlight the shared designation and the tagged posts will automatically be shared with your students. Any tags that have been shared with you will also show up in this section.

Creating and editing assignments (Intermediate)

Go paperless in your classroom with this feature. You can upload documents, link videos, and assign due dates to help keep your students on track.

Getting ready

Create the assignment via a Word document and prepare to upload it to Edmodo.

How to do it...

Quit copying papers to hand out and create an online assignment by following these steps:

1. Click on **Assignment**.
2. Name the assignment.
3. Type an overview of the assignment in the description box.
4. Attach any file or link.
5. Determine a due date.
6. Send to the appropriate group/groups.

How it works...

Assignments can be posted, downloaded, and graded with ease through Edmodo. Simply create your assignment via a Word document or with another online tool. When you are ready, click on **Assignment** on your main Edmodo page in the **Post** section. If this is the first time you are creating an assignment in Edmodo, you will need to designate an assignment title. Tab down to the next field and include a written description of the assignment. There is no character limit in this field, so feel free to be as descriptive as needed. Tab down to the next field to list the assignment due date. This due date will automatically be exported into your Edmodo calendar. At this juncture, if you have created an additional file with the assignment content, you may upload the file by clicking on the **File** icon. This will take you to your computer filing system where you can choose one or more files to upload. You may also click on the **Link** icon to designate any external web links that are necessary for the assignment completion.

If you have content in your Edmodo Library, it is possible to also attach any of that content to the Edmodo assignment. The process for adding Edmodo Library content to your assignment requires you to click on the **Library** icon. Once you are in your Edmodo Library, simply choose the appropriate file that contains the necessary content. Highlight one or more documents in the file and click on **Attach**.

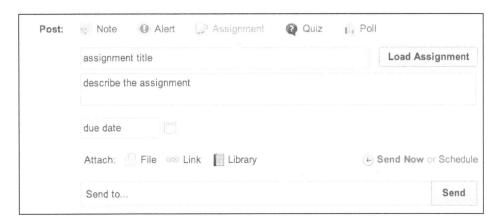

Similar to posting a note, you can schedule the assignment. If you are creating the assignment the day in which you intend the students to see the assignment, it is acceptable to post the assignment immediately. However, if you are working ahead and do not want your students to have access to the assignment, please schedule your post for the appropriate date and time in which you intend students to have access to it. To schedule the post, you will take the same steps as you did for scheduling a note. Click on **Schedule** in the lower right-hand corner of the **Assignment** tab. Choose the appropriate date and time in which you want the assignment to become visible to the students. These scheduled assignments will now show up in your **Notifications** section as a scheduled post, and can be accessed by clicking on the yellow **Notifications** tab on the upper right-hand side of your Edmodo home screen. The plus symbol will expand this section and reveal your scheduled posts. Simply click on the scheduled post in this area, if you wish to review the assignment.

To send the assignment, whether immediately or in the future, type the group name or individual names of group members to designate the recipients of the assignment. Thus, just like in the posting of a note or a poll, multiple groups or multiple group members can receive the same assignment. Once you have the chosen recipients, simply click on Send. Remember, if it is a scheduled assignment to be posted in the future, the recipients will not receive the assignment until the scheduled date and time. It is also a good practice to send the same assignment out to each group individually if you do not want possible comments from all of the groups to show up on the assignment. I don't mind sending my assignments out to all groups at once to save time. I also like that a member in one group may have a question that could benefit a member in a different group. However, this could also be a drawback if you don't want members from multiple groups interacting. If this is the case, simply send the assignment separately to each group.

There's more...

Once you have created an assignment in Edmodo, you will never need to recreate that same assignment.

Recreating an assignment

Click on **Assignment** on your main Edmodo home page in the Post section. This is the same process you took to create the initial assignment. However, instead of creating a new assignment, you will now click on **Load Assignment**. This will take you to a screen that lists all assignments that you have previously created. Simply choose the appropriate assignment you wish to upload and click on the assignment name. This will automatically autopopulate the assignment title and assignment description fields in the **Assignment** section. Once these fields have been autopopulated, you may make any edits that you wish. You will still have to choose to upload any external documents, Edmodo Library documents, or web links. You will still have to choose the due date and the groups to whom you intend to send the assignment.

Grading an assignment

Once you have created and sent the assignment to the appropriate groups, the assignment will now show up on the main Edmodo wall for the designated groups. As the owner of the group, you will be able to see the number of group members who have turned in the assignment. This will help you visually monitor the group's progress on the assignment.

By clicking on the **Turned in** icon, you will be redirected to a split screen that lists the students on the left-hand side and the assignment on the right-hand side. On the right-hand side of the screen, you will want to fill in the points for the assignment in the empty box beside **Set Default Total**. This will then autopopulate the point total for each student when you are ready to grade the assignment.

The student list will indicate which students have turned in the assignment with a green, **Turned in** designation. You may grade the assignment from this screen. To do so, simply click on the appropriate student. The right-hand side of your split screen will now contain the turned in assignment from that student. Read the assignment contents typed in the comment section and download any documents. Assign the earned points that will automatically be uploaded on your Edmodo gradebook. Refer to the *Using the Edmodo gradebook (Intermediate)* recipe for additional information on the gradebook feature.

Creating quizzes (Intermediate)

Create a multiple choice, short answer, true or false, fill in the blank, or matching quiz that can be shared to multiple classes and scored by Edmodo. The results will be displayed as a graph to help you determine any deficient areas of learning.

Getting ready

Determine what type of quiz questions will be most effective in order to assess your students' understanding of the significant content in question.

How to do it...

Create your quizzes that Edmodo will automatically grade by performing the following steps:

1. Click on **Quiz**.
2. Click on **Create a Quiz**.
3. Title your quiz.
4. Set a time limit.
5. Choose your type of question.
6. Add questions.
7. Assign the quiz.

How it works...

Click on **Create a Quiz** in the **Post** section of your Edmodo home page. Click on the **Create a Quiz** icon that now appears on your screen. On the top left-hand side of the screen to which you have been directed, you will need to delete the automatically generated title of your quiz. Type in your new title of the quiz you are creating. Now, you need to type in a set time limit that you deem to be appropriate for your quiz.

You have the option of using **Multiple Choice**, **Short Answer**, **True/False**, **Fill in the Blank**, or **Matching** questions. These choices are listed in the drop-down menu beside **Type:**. Then, click on **Add First Question**. The type of question you pick will determine the way in which you add the content of the question. For instance, a multiple-choice question will provide you with a space to add the various possible responses for the students to choose. However, if you create a short-answer question, the student responses will vary and you will not have the option to type in a response to be automatically scored by Edmodo. For the multiple-choice, true/false, and matching questions, you will need to designate the correct answer for automatic scoring purposes. For the fill in the blank type, you will need to type in an underscore (_) at the appropriate point in which you intend the blank value in the question to appear. Underneath the section where you are typing the question, a box will appear for you to insert the correct answer.

Question Prompt:	Use '_' **underscores** to specify where you would like a blank to appear in the text below.

You must wear a "_____" outside when it is cold.

Attach: ⚗ Link   📄 Library

You must wear a " coat " outside when it is cold.

You have the option to show students the results of their quiz and to randomize the questions to prevent possible cheating in the quiz. You need to check the appropriate boxes on the lower right-hand side of your **Question Prompt:** screen to ensure either of these.

To preview your quiz, click on the **Preview** button located on the right-hand side of your quiz screen. You will be able to view the quiz as if you were a student taking the quiz. At the conclusion of the quiz, you will see your results and will be able to assign an emoticon to show your reaction to the quiz. This preview mode makes you a student of the class and the view will be as if you are a student. To end the preview mode, click on **End Preview** at the top of screen that is highlighted in yellow. Once you are satisfied with the preview and no edits are necessary, you may now assign the quiz. The blue box in the top right-hand corner of the screen will assign the quiz.

Now that you have assigned the quiz, you still need to set a due date and send the quiz to the appropriate groups. You also have the option of automatically adding the quiz grade to your Edmodo gradebook. To do this, check the **Add to Gradebook** selection on your screen. Additionally, just as you had the option to schedule an assignment or a note, you may do so as well with a quiz. Once the quiz has fully been assigned, similar to the assignment feature, you will see the number of students who have turned in their quiz. Clicking on the turned in portion of the quiz will take you to the split screen with the students on the left and the quiz on the right. From this screen, you can view the students who have taken the quiz and their scores.

Once you have created a quiz, just as you can with the assignment feature, you are able to load a previously-created quiz. This previously-created quiz can be edited. However, please note that an edited quiz will be titled as a copy of the original quiz. It is also possible to load previously-created questions. This feature can be seen in the first screenshot of this section. You can also choose to print a copy of a created quiz for students who require a printed version for necessary adaptations.

There's more...

Your automatically-graded quizzes in Edmodo will provide you with visual results of the quiz that can be quickly analyzed.

Viewing quiz results

Once all students have completed their assigned quiz, you can click on the turned in portion of the quiz post to see the results. Edmodo provides you with the average score. To see this, hover over the perpendicular bar on the **Average score** section at the top of the split screen on the right. A percentage will be given. Next to the **Average score** section, the red and green horizontal lines will provide you with a status of the students who have completed the quiz. The red portion signifies any student who has not completed the quiz. Again, hovering over the red will tell you the number of students who have yet to complete the quiz. An all-green line indicates all students have completed the quiz.

The results of the individual questions are shown on the right-hand side of the split screen as a pie chart. Hovering over each pie chart provides the data of the number of students who missed the question. The red portion of the chart is indicative of those students who missed the question. With each question, an emoticon average is also provided. Thus, if a particular question that is written is confusing or students weren't prepared for the question, feedback is provided to ensure reflection on the part of the teacher.

Using the Edmodo gradebook (Intermediate)

Now that you have mastered creating assignments and quizzes in Edmodo, scoring them will be easy. The use of the Edmodo gradebook will give parents and students immediate online access to their class standings and progress.

Getting ready

Now that you have created assignments and quizzes in Edmodo, you have already been adding to your Edmodo gradebook without even knowing it!

How to do it...

You automatically enter grades in Edmodo when you score student assignments and quizzes.

1. Create assignments and quizzes in Edmodo.
2. Click on the gradebook.
3. View student results.

How it works...

Hover over the notebook with a checkmark icon on the top left-hand side of your Edmodo home page screen. All assignments and quizzes that have been created in Edmodo will automatically appear as long as you have selected **Add to Gradebook** when the assignment or quiz was created. Since the quizzes are automatically graded, these grades will be added as soon as the student submits the quiz. The assignments will need to be graded by you. You can grade the assignments as previously described, or you can click on the assignments from within the Edmodo gradebook and then follow the steps described previously.

If you want to add a grade that is not linked to an Edmodo assignment or quiz, such as a participation grade, you can click on **New Grade** on the top left-hand side of the gradebook screen. Title your new grade and set the default total points. Then click on **Create Grade**. At this point, you will have to manually enter the grades by tabbing through the gradebook.

You can view the work from each assignment that a student submits when in the gradebook. Simply click on the chosen grade and then click on **View Work**. This will take you to the assignment submission screen described in the *Creating and editing assignments* recipe.

There's more...

If you want to recognize students' achievements and create an online atmosphere of motivation, think about going beyond simple grades earned. Creating and awarding badges on Edmodo can have a positive impact on your students' academic and online behavior.

Creating badges

When in the gradebook view in Edmodo, click on **Badges** at the top left-hand side of the screen. Then click on **Add a Badge to this Group**. You can choose from several badges already created by Edmodo to assign to a student. These include **Hard Worker**, **Star Performer**, and **Good Question** among others. You also have the ability to create your own badges.

To create your own badge, click on **New Badge** located on the left-hand side of the screen. Create a badge title and a written description of the badge. Then you need to upload a picture that will represent the badge. Please note that you should practice and model good online citizenship by using an image that is copyright free. You may also choose to share the newly-created badge with other teachers by checking the **Share with other teachers** checkbox. This box is autopopulated with a check, so be sure to uncheck the checkbox if you don't want to share your badge. Once your badge is created, you can assign it to your students.

To add badges to individual students, you first need to add the badge to the group. To do this, click on the chosen badge, either Edmodo-created or your own, and then click on **Add badge to this Group**. Once the badge has been added to the group, you may assign it to any student. All badges assigned to the group are listed horizontally at the top of your badge section of your gradebook. To add a badge to a student, click on the cell under the badge that corresponds to the appropriate student. You can see the total number of badges earned by a student as listed next to their name.

Managing your Edmodo planner (Simple)

You don't have to worry about students forgetting to write assignment due dates in their planner anymore. Edmodo creates an easy-to-use and easy-to-reference planner for teachers, students, and parents.

Getting ready

Your planner has been automatically generated as you have created assignments in Edmodo, but you have the ability to customize it even further.

How to do it...

An Edmodo Planner is easily created to help students and teachers manage their calendar. You can add tasks or events with their schedules to your planner by performing the following steps:

1. Create Edmodo assignments.
2. Add new tasks.
3. Create events.
4. View by week or by month.

How it works...

Edmodo manages the day-to-day classroom activities, assignments, and quizzes in an easy-to-read, color-coded calendar that is automatically generated once you create content with due dates. This means for each assignment you build on Edmodo, you will find the corresponding due date when you click on the planner symbol on the top left-hand corner of the Edmodo home screen. Clicking on this icon will take you to a weekly view of these due dates. Notice the visual ease of recognizing the assignment that pertains to the corresponding group based on the assigned group color. To see a monthly view of the planner, click on the tab for month on the left-hand side of the screen just above the planner.

You may also choose to view your planner by a particular group only. To eliminate viewing the planner content of all the groups you manage, look at the top left-hand side of your screen for **Everything** that is in a blue box. Click on the box to drill down and select the specific group you would like to view as a singular entity on the planner. All other events on the planner will be eliminated from your view. To return to the view with all events from all groups included, change the blue box back to **Everything**.

To add content to the planner, click on the **New Task** tab located on the right-hand side of your planner screen. Type a description of the task and designate the appropriate due date. Click on **Create** and you will see that the task has been added to your planner. These tasks are a great way for you to manage your to-do list as a teacher. These tasks are not sent to a particular group and cannot be viewed by them.

You may also create new events by following the same process as for new tasks. The **Events** tab is located to the left of the **New Task** tab. Click on the **Events** tab and type a description of the event. You may choose to designate a specific date, or you may want to use a date range if the event will span more than a day. The event may be sent to one or more groups and will be typed into the **Send to...** field. The event may also be sent to individual group members if you choose.

To edit or delete any tasks or events on your planner, click on the designated task to be changed. An editable field will appear on your screen. Make the appropriate changes from here or click on **Delete this task**. If you have completed the task, in order to manage your to-do list, click on **Completed task** in the editable field. Now your task will show up in your planner with a check mark next to it to indicate that it has been completed.

There's more...

You may need to complete future planning that you aren't quite ready to add to a specific date in your planner.

Planning ahead

When you are in the weekly view of the planner, you will notice two fields at the bottom of the screen. The right-hand side lists **COMING SOON** and includes events and assignments for the upcoming week. On the left-hand side, there is a field to add future events to **SOMEDAY**. You may add tasks that you intend to complete in the future, but aren't ready to add to your planner. Click on the **New Task** icon in this portion of your screen. Add the description of the task and click on **Create**. This will begin your list of tasks that you don't want to forget and will add to your planner in the future. To add additional tasks, you will now need to click on the plus mark icon on the far right of the **SOMEDAY** field.

Managing your Edmodo Library (Intermediate)

Maintain a virtual record of all of your documents, links, and videos in your Edmodo Library. Learn how to organize your content and share it with others.

Getting ready

Choose the content you would like to share with your groups. Determine how you would like to organize it.

How to do it...

An online Library manages files and links for personal use and sharing with group members.

1. Click on the **Book** icon.
2. Create a new folder.
3. Add to library by clicking on **Add to Library**.
4. Share to groups.

How it works...

Click on the **Book** icon located on the top left-hand side of your Edmodo home screen. At the top-left of this screen you will see the **Add to Library** tab. Click on this tab and upload either a file from your computer or attach a link from the Internet. Once the file has been uploaded, click on **Add**. To attach the Internet link, first click on **Link** and then copy and paste the URL into the embed tab. The title of the Internet page will automatically appear below the pasted URL. Click on **Add** to include the link in your Library.

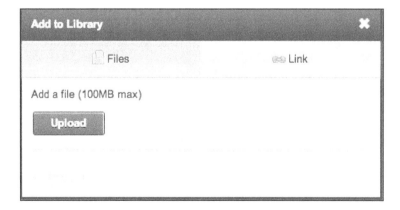

To organize your Library items, click on the **New** tab on the left-hand side of your Library screen. This will create a new folder. Type in a name for the newly created folder and click on **Create**. To add a file or link to the folder, click on the item to highlight it. You can now view that item on the right-hand side of the split screen. Click on the **Folder** tab at the bottom of the item. A list of all of the folders in your Library will appear. Check the appropriate folder or folders with which you would like to include the link or file. Then click on the blue-colored **Apply** tab. If you have an extensive list of folders, rather than scrolling down the list, you can also search for the folder by typing the name of the folder in the search bar from the same screen.

The list of your folders is located on the left-hand side of your Library screen. Choose the appropriate folder to view. Items in the folder may be organized by dragging-and-dropping into a particular order. The items may also be highlighted and then launched in play view. Clicking on the **Launched in Play View** tab will bring up the file or link for you to view. To return to the Library, simply click on **Back to library**.

To share a folder with a group, click on the designated folder. At the top of this view, click on the **People** icon to choose the group with which you intend to share the folder. Check the group or groups to automatically share the folder with. You may also choose to make the folder public by checking this designation at the top of this screen view. To leave this sharing view, just click anywhere on your screen outside sharing view.

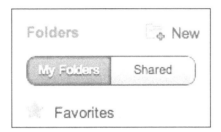

The gear icon located just to the right of the people icon will allow you to delete or edit the name of your folder. If you choose to delete the folder, a **Delete Folder** view will appear. You will be asked to confirm your desire to delete the folder.

When folders are shared with you by another group, the list will appear on the left-hand side of your Library screen next to your **My Folders** list. Click on **Shared** to see this list of shared folders and items. All of your shared Library items can be filtered at the top of the Library home screen. The **Filter by type** tab will provide a drop-down list from which you can choose the items to be filtered. The default is All types and includes both the Internet links and files, which have been uploaded. To sort the two, choose the appropriate designation for either links or files. In the same area, it is also possible to choose to view a list of all items in your Library or to view them as a matrix. The most recently added Library item will appear at the head of the list or at the top of the matrix, with the last item being identified as the one that was added first.

There's more...

If you haven't intentionally added a link or file to your Edmodo Library, but have shared these with one of your Edmodo groups, you can still easily search for these items. Additionally, documents that you have already created via your Google Drive account can be easily linked to your Edmodo Library.

Automatically added Library items

Any links and files that you have been attaching to your Edmodo notes are automatically added to your Library. To see these items, click on **Attached to Posts** located on the top left-hand side of your screen. These are not items that you have added to your Library, but rather were added by Edmodo. The items are automatically sorted. Click on the group with whom you had originally shared the item to see this. To find the group, click on the blue-colored **All Groups** tab and use the drop-down menu to find the desired group name.

Google Drive and the Edmodo Library

If you have been using Google Drive to create documents, you do not need to download the document to your computer and upload it to Edmodo in order to share it with your groups. Edmodo has eliminated this need by creating a shortcut to connect your two accounts. To do this, click on the **Book** icon to take you to the Library view in Edmodo. On the left-hand side of the screen, click on the **Google Docs** tab. Since your Google account has not been linked to Edmodo prior to this point, you will see a large **Connect with Google Docs** tab. Click on this tab. You will be taken to a Google screen that asks for your permission to connect the two accounts. By allowing access, Edmodo may view and manage any of your documents and files in Google Drive. You may choose to not allow Edmodo this access. If you decide not to allow the access, you can still download a file from Google Drive and then upload it into your Edmodo Library. However, by allowing Edmodo this access, you skip these steps and save time. You may also disconnect Edmodo's access to your Google Drive account at any time. To do this, in the **Google Docs** view of your Edmodo Library, click on the **Disconnect Account** tab on the right-hand side of your screen.

edmodo is requesting permission to:

▸ View and manage any of your documents and files in Google Drive

▸ View and manage any of your documents and files in Google Drive

▸ View and manage your spreadsheets in Google Drive

◦ Perform these operations when I'm not using the application

Allow access   No thanks

Creating parent accounts in Edmodo (Intermediate)

Giving parents access to your classroom's group creates a connected experience for them. Parent accounts are automatically linked to the appropriate students by Edmodo, so take advantage of this feature.

Getting ready

Parents can create a parent account in Edmodo at `http://www.edmodo.com`.

How to do it...

Encouraging parent access to Edmodo is advisable. Parents can connect to their student's classrom groups by performing the following steps:

1. Create a parent account.
2. Teacher provides a unique parent code.
3. Parents can now view group activity.

How it works...

Each student in your Edmodo groups has a unique parent code that is already generated by Edmodo. This code can be found in two places. From the student's account, on the right-hand side of the Edmodo home page, a box with the parent code is displayed. Students are directed to provide this code to their parents for access to Edmodo. From your teacher account, select the appropriate group from the left-hand side of your screen. Select the **Members** tab from the top-center of your screen. Click on the **Printer** icon and select **Parent Codes** from the drop-down menu. The parent code list will automatically be downloaded to your computer. Parent codes can be appropriately distributed based on any communication method you deem appropriate. If you need to find the parent code for one student only and do not need to download the codes for all students, simply click on the **Members** tab at the top-center of your group's home page. Click on the selected student. This student's information will appear in a split screen on the right-hand side of your page. The parent code may be retrieved from this spot by clicking on **Parent Code**.

Once parents have created their accounts, you will be able to click on the **People** icon on the top-right of this same screen. The parents who have registered and joined the group will be displayed here.

In order to create their accounts, from the Edmodo home page, parents register to create a parent account. Parents must enter the unique six-digit code associated with their child. Parents must also designate the relationship they have with the student in question. The rest of the registration process mirrors that of the student registration. A parent's first and last names, password, and e-mail address are all required to complete the registration process. Parents must also agree to the terms of service and privacy policy for Edmodo.

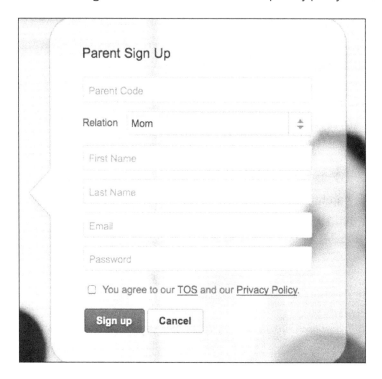

Once a parent has signed up for Edmodo, they will be automatically linked to any groups with which their student is associated. This means a group that a student joins in the future will also be connected to the parent's account. Parents have access to the grades received by their students. You can also send parents a message on Edmodo. Follow the process for creating a note and choose the parents to whom you would like to send the note.

Participating in Edmodo communities (Intermediate)

Use Edmodo to help you grow your personal learning network. Connect with your subject area and then find additional communities of interest with which you can engage to find resources, share ideas, and receive feedback on your work.

Getting ready

Expand the number of teachers with whom you collaborate by joining Edmodo communities.

1. Click on **Communities**.
2. Choose the desired communities you wish to join.

How to do it...

Click on the **Communities** tab located on the lower-left corner of your screen. This is located just under your **Groups** that you have already established. You will notice that you have already been automatically enrolled in the **Help** community, which is designated by a question mark symbol.

How it works...

If you haven't done so already, you have the option of joining the Edmodo-created communities. These communities relate to specific content areas. So, if you are a Health and P.E. teacher, you will want to join this community. The communities are an excellent place to find and post resources, share ideas, and make connections with educators who may be interested in partnering for a collaborative project between several Groups of students. The **Professional Development** community is also a must for any new teacher to Edmodo. This community provides a wealth of ideas for classroom management, lesson development, and educational Web 2.0 tools for classroom implementation. Edmodo will also automatically enroll you in the **Help** community that is indicated by a red, question mark symbol. The Help community provides continuous online support from the Edmodo help team of experts. If you have a question, notice a system bug, or have a suggestion for improvements, this is the place to go. Post a note and within a short period of time, someone from the help team will respond to your inquiry.

Once you've completed your profile, you will also have the opportunity to join other publisher communities that have been established by outside organizations or interests. You can find these communities by browsing the selections. Options include **Kahn Academy**, **Voice Thread**, **Mathalicious**, and nearly 200 other educator-related groups that may pique your interest. These publisher communities are not Edmodo-created, but have many of the same functionalities of the Edmodo communities. They also provide the potential to connect with thousands of other teachers on common topics and interests.

There's more...

Once you are a member of these communities, you may communicate and share resources with other community members.

Commenting in the communities

To comment on a resource or post within the community, follow the same steps as listed in the *Posting on the Edmodo wall (Simple)* recipe. If you find a teacher within the community with whom you would like to make a further connection, click on the teacher's name. This will take you to the profile for that teacher. Once in the profile screen, click on the green tab, **Add Connection**, in the upper right-hand side of the screen. Once the teacher accepts the connection, you are now able to send direct messages to that teacher using the same steps described in the *Posting on the Edmodo wall (Simple)* recipe.

Adding community content to your Library

You can add content from a community to your Library. Click on the **Add to Library** icon that is located next to the designated link or document that has been posted in the community news feed. The most used content in the community is located on the right-hand side panel of the community home page. This is listed as **Trending Community Content**.

Using Edmodo apps (Advanced)

The basic functions of Edmodo are free. Once you've mastered the ins and outs of the tools, you may be ready for the more advanced, paid offerings that can be downloaded from the Edmodo app store.

Getting ready

Browse the apps store to determine which apps may be of use to you in your classroom.

How to do it...

Expand your Edmodo usage by purchasing Edmodo app credit.

1. Click on the **Apps** icon.
2. Go to the store by clicking on **Go to Store**.
3. Purchase selected apps.

How it works...

Click on the **Apps** icon located on the top left-hand side of your Edmodo home page. Click on **Go to Store**. From this screen you may choose to browse both the paid and free apps. Edmodo also suggests several possible apps for your use, as well as lists apps by category that relates to your subject area. When you find an app that may be of your interest, click on the app logo. This screen will detail more information about the app and will provide several screenshots of the app for further investigation. At this juncture, you may wish to purchase the app or add it to your wishlist. Each app lists a purchase price. For some apps, the purchase price is unlimited for the number of groups to which you link the app. For other apps, you will pay a per-group price. To purchase, click on the groups for which you want to use the app and agree to the **End User Agreement**. Then click on **Install**.

In order to add money to your Edmodo account, click on **Purchase Credit**. Choose the amount of credit you would like to add to your account. Click on the blue box, **Next: Payment Method**. Enter your credit card information and review your purchase. The credit in your Edmodo account is good toward the purchase of any app.

Once you have added apps to your Edmodo groups, you are able to manage the apps. Again, click on the **Apps** icon located on the top left-hand side of your Edmodo home page. From this screen, click on **Manage My Apps**. You may filter the apps by the groups in which they are installed. Click on the app icon that you desire. On this page you will see a description of the app and the groups in which you have installed the app. On the right-hand side of the split screen, you may select any groups for which you intend to uninstall the app. Simply click on "x" to the right of the group. Edmodo will ask you to confirm that you want to uninstall the app.

There's more...

Now that you've installed your selected apps, it is time to begin using them with your Edmodo groups.

App account information

Each app you install will require you to create an account. Click on that app to begin using the app. The app will depend on the way in which you use it with your groups.

About Packt Publishing

Packt, pronounced 'packed', published its first book "*Mastering phpMyAdmin for Effective MySQL Management*" in April 2004 and subsequently continued to specialize in publishing highly focused books on specific technologies and solutions.

Our books and publications share the experiences of your fellow IT professionals in adapting and customizing today's systems, applications, and frameworks. Our solution based books give you the knowledge and power to customize the software and technologies you're using to get the job done. Packt books are more specific and less general than the IT books you have seen in the past. Our unique business model allows us to bring you more focused information, giving you more of what you need to know, and less of what you don't.

Packt is a modern, yet unique publishing company, which focuses on producing quality, cutting-edge books for communities of developers, administrators, and newbies alike. For more information, please visit our website: www.packtpub.com.

Writing for Packt

We welcome all inquiries from people who are interested in authoring. Book proposals should be sent to author@packtpub.com. If your book idea is still at an early stage and you would like to discuss it first before writing a formal book proposal, contact us; one of our commissioning editors will get in touch with you.

We're not just looking for published authors; if you have strong technical skills but no writing experience, our experienced editors can help you develop a writing career, or simply get some additional reward for your expertise.

Moodle Gradebook

ISBN: 978-1-849518-14-7   Paperback: 128 pages

Set up and customize the gradebook to track student progress through Moodle

1. Use Moodle's powerful gradebook more effectively to monitor and report on the progress of your students

2. Customize the gradebook to calculate and show the information you need

3. Discover new grading features and tracking functions now available in Moodle 2

Moodle 2.0 Course Conversion Beginner's Guide

ISBN: 978-1-849514-82-8   Paperback: 368 pages

A complete guide to successful learning using Moodle 2.0

1. Move your existing course notes, worksheets, and resources into Moodle quickly

2. No need to start from scratch! This book shows you the quickest way to start using Moodle and e-learning, by bringing your existing lesson materials into Moodle

3. Demonstrates quick ways to improve your course, taking advantage of multimedia and collaboration

Please check **www.PacktPub.com** for information on our titles

Instant Moodle Quiz Module How-to

ISBN: 978-1-849519-88-5   Paperback: 84 pages

Create Moodle quizzes to enhance learning using practical, hands-on recipes

1. Learn something new in an Instant! A short, fast, focused guide delivering immediate results

2. Create a well categorized question bank to provide the foundation for quizzes

3. Provide extensive learner-centred feedback to enhance learning

4. Use reports to analyze learner results

Moodle 2 for Teaching 7-14 Year Olds Beginner's Guide

ISBN: 978-1-849518-32-1   Paperback: 258 pages

Effective e-learning for younger students, using Moodle as your classroom assistant

1. Ideal for teachers new to Moodle: easy to follow and abundantly illustrated with screenshots of the solutions you'll build

2. Go paperless! Put your lessons online and grade them anywhere, anytime

3. Engage and motivate your students with games, quizzes, movies, blogs, and podcasts the whole class can participate in

Please check **www.PacktPub.com** for information on our titles